T0381457

Also by Barbara Bryant

Compensated Suffering
Gifted Inspirations
Stedmon Makes Me Laugh & I Make Him Pray
F.B.I. (Favor, Blessings, Increase)
I'm Not Every Woman

THE PROMISES OF MILK AND HONEY

Rediscover the One Who Keeps His Words

BARBARA BRYANT

WESTBOW PRESS®
A DIVISION OF THOMAS NELSON
& ZONDERVAN

This book is a work of non-fiction. Unless otherwise noted, the author and the publisher make no explicit guarantees as to the accuracy of the information contained in this book and in some cases, names of people and places have been altered to protect their privacy.

WestBow Press books may be ordered through booksellers or by contacting:

WestBow Press
A Division of Thomas Nelson & Zondervan
1663 Liberty Drive
Bloomington, IN 47403
www.westbowpress.com
844-714-3454

Because of the dynamic nature of the Internet, any web addresses or links contained in this book may have changed since publication and may no longer be valid. The views expressed in this work are solely those of the author and do not necessarily reflect the views of the publisher, and the publisher hereby disclaims any responsibility for them.

Any people depicted in stock imagery provided by Getty Images are models, and such images are being used for illustrative purposes only. Certain stock imagery © Getty Images.

ISBN: 979-8-3850-3153-5 (sc)
ISBN: 979-8-3850-3155-9 (hc)
ISBN: 979-8-3850-3154-2 (e)

Library of Congress Control Number: 2024916637

Print information available on the last page.

WestBow Press rev. date: 09/03/2024

CONTENTS

DEDICATION

This book is dedicated to my beloved grandchildren, Sophia, Sloane and Steven Christopher Tillman whose laughter is my favorite sound. It is my prayer that they might one day use it to remind themselves how important it is to stand on the promises of God.

To my sons, Steven and Stedmon, who continue to inspire me to teach sermons and tell stories that matter.

To my two daughters-in-law, Shanita and Sarah who fill my heart with joy each day.

To the ones reading this, may you find the courage, joy, love and promises of God contained within these pages.

To myself, for showing up, pushing through, and finishing what I started, which was this book.

FOREWORD

Our great God will announce to an overlooked shepherd that he will become a king. A couple advanced in age will conceive a child. Frustrated fishermen who are willing to launch in faith will be fruitful in their endeavors. You haven't walked in thirty-eight years; you can today. And yes, a virgin who has not consummated a marriage can conceive a son. These life-changing stories speak to the transformational power of God's Word, which needs no external ingredients for affirmations, only a committed person's faith and trust in a God who cannot fail. We serve a God who calls those things that are not as if they were.

If there is anyone qualified to speak on this journey of faith, it is Dr. Barbara Bryant. She is a woman who is fully aware that the announcements of God's plans of greatness in our lives will rarely be accompanied by ideal circumstances. Setbacks, self-doubt, and sabotage will be landmines on the path of promise. However, they will only serve as trainers that forge our faith and test our acts of obedience as we walk out God's will.

In this landmark book, *The Promises of Milk and Honey*, Dr. Bryant shares the necessary life principles, strategies, and character development that it will take to lay hold of the prize that has been set before us. Dr. Bryant is a qualified instructor whom we have all witnessed in her diligent submission to the Master's call and God's faithfulness in His word to her. She has raised two sons, given birth to a ministry, authored several books, recorded music, served her local church, and pursued a professional career while proclaiming the power of our Savior. Her life is a shining example to women of all ages and economic backgrounds of what can be done to a heart that will yield to Christ.

Do you sense the Father's hand upon your life, His call to a greater purpose and design for you? Might you be surrounded by a checkered past, with few encouraging family and friends, and self-doubt in your redeemable qualities and skills? Take courage, my brother and my sister. God's Word cannot lie, and what He has spoken will come to pass. Read this book prayerfully, with an open heart to hear instructions for your eternity, for you are holding in your hands the manual to milk and honey.

Pastor Phillip White
The Regenerated Church
Los Angeles, California

A LETTER FROM BARBARA BRYANT

Guided by the wisdom of the Lord, I write this book to remind men and women that God gives us promises. Promises from God are statements of His will and purpose for His people. However, the promise is linked to a principle (or condition), followed by a problem (temptation in the wilderness), leading to His provision (milk and honey). The fulfillment of the promise may take some time, but believe it's coming. For example, Abraham was seventy-five years old when God made the promise that he would be the father of a multitude of nations. For twenty-five years, he continued to believe in the promise of God, even though his physical body was withering away every single day. Yet Abraham believed God, and the promise came to pass.

The Scripture is full of powerful stories of the Lord's promises being established in the lives of people, sometimes years after the initial giving of the promise. There are literally thousands of scriptures in the Bible that can be applied to our lives, because everything God offers comes in promise form. As a Christian, you have an inheritance from the Lord. Since you are "in Christ," you are an heir to all the promises God made to Abraham. As an heir, you don't have to do anything to receive your inheritance. When you were born again, you were born into Jesus and the family of God.

Two of the promises that are part of your inheritance are milk and honey. The "land of milk and honey" served as a powerful biblical metaphor for abundance, fertility, and prosperity. Together, they represent a place of great blessing. God promises to provide milk and honey to His chosen people as a sign of His provision.

The process by which you enter your inheritance is like the journey made by the Israelites to the Promised Land: step by step, stage by stage, season by season. The journey will not be easy, but in the end, you will discover that God keeps His Word.

In this treatise, we are going to search for answers to those desperate questions. I will give you a hint: part of the answer is that we have been so often disappointed that it is difficult to believe in a new paradigm. However, that is not the way we are supposed to live. So let us change things up.

First, let's review marvelous promises that guided the writing for this book.

> So I have come down to deliver them from the power of the Egyptians, and to bring them up from that land to a good and spacious land, to a land flowing with milk and honey. (Exodus 3:8 NASB)

We can take the Father at His Word, because His Word is true, and He does not change. He is who He is, and He does what He has said He will do. He has all the wisdom and power needed to execute His promises for His children. As the psalmist wrote, "For He spoke, and it was done; He commanded, and it stood fast" (Psalm 33:9 NKJV). Realize that God has given us specific promises to remind us that the land of milk and honey is for us.

Enjoy this inspiring read. *The Promises of Milk and Honey* will prepare your heart to believe and receive the promises of God.

Get ready for milk and honey,
Barbara Bryant

CHAPTER 1

Promise Guaranteed

"Promises, promises." No doubt you've heard this phrase uttered with sarcasm because the speaker is unsure of the validity of promises after being often disappointed. Broken promises hurt. A broken promise can bring disappointment, distrust, and sadness. A broken promise has the potential to sever relationships, bring heartache, and wound deeply.

People will disappoint us and let us down. We may hear a person say, "I know I promised, but I'm sorry, I can't do what I promised." There is anger at the promise-breaker and shame that we trusted them. We lash out, crawl away, or pretend we didn't really care. Why? Broken promises, big or small, corrode trust. And without trust in a relationship, there is no feeling of emotional safety. Do not add to the pain of your blame; take comfort in the character of God.

You can trust the promises found in the Word of God—they are solid and immense, and we can stand on them forever (Luke 6:47–48). The Lord is not negligent in fulfilling His promises. When He makes a promise, He keeps it. He is the only one in the universe who is a loyal and reliable promise keeper. So what is it that He promises? We can expect all the promises of the Lord to be yes and amen in Christ! His

1

promises are guaranteed. God has seen fit to confirm His promises with an oath.

> When God made his promise to Abraham, since there was no one greater for him to swear by, he swore upon himself, saying, "Blessing I will bless you, and multiplying I will multiply your descendants…" (Genesis 22:17 KJV) And so after waiting patiently, Abraham received what was promised. (Hebrews 6:13–15 NIV)

While this message was originally meant for persecuted Jewish Christians, the theme is relevant to all believers. The author is not trying to connect you to your dreams but to God's. He wants you to know the promise God made to Abraham is one Christians are recipients of today. We are meant to believe the promise Abraham believed. If we understand the promise God made to Abraham, we will have an anchor for our lives today.

The promises from God became ours at the moment of our salvation, so we would have everything we need for life and godliness. God's promises not only remind us of His care and love for us, but also provide hope and encouragement during tough times.

> A biblical promise is a declaration of
> God's intention to graciously bestow a gift
> on an individual or a group of people.

Promises are not given without a plan that involves faith and responsibility, though many times we must wait for the promises to be revealed. A biblical promise is a declaration of God's intention to graciously bestow a gift on an individual or a group of people.

When God promises something, it will always come to pass, even if it takes a long time. No matter how long you've been waiting, something is coming for you as a believer. God guarantees it. You can take it to the bank. God is so certain about it, so determined to do it, and so committed to His own purposes that He made a "deposit" in us that guarantees "what is to come." This promise is found in 2 Corinthians 5:5 (NIV): "Now the one who has fashioned us for this very purpose is God, who has given us the Spirit as a deposit, guaranteeing what is to come."

The Christian life sometimes includes long waits for the fulfillment of God's promises. Nevertheless, God will fulfill the words that He spoke over your life. Many times, when we don't see God's promises over our lives manifest, we want to give up and move on. Disappointment sets in, and we want to stop believing because it hurts. Then, to top it off, we have been conditioned by the world that we can get things instantly, and we assume that God works that way. God keeps His promises, and although we may not see them manifest immediately, we can trust that He is at work in our lives.

God will complete His work, but God sometimes fulfills His promises in ways we could never have imagined. At times, the Lord has used methods we can easily understand. He sent His people into battle with a promise of victory, and He gave them strength and strategy to overcome their enemies. On other occasions, He did the unexpected. He defeated Pharaoh's army as they pursued the escaping Israelites (Exodus 14). He caused the walls of Jericho to collapse (Joshua 6). The angel of the Lord destroyed 185,000 Assyrians (2 Kings 19:35). God will sometimes fulfill His promises in unexpected and supernatural ways.

While we try to figure out how God is going to answer a prayer or fulfill His promises, He is powerfully working out His plans behind the scenes and in ways that we may not comprehend. It should not surprise us that in the book of Isaiah, the Lord described our inability to understand His methods: "'For my thoughts are not your thoughts, neither are your ways my ways,' declares the Lord. 'As the heavens are higher than the earth, so are my ways higher than your ways and my thoughts than your thoughts'" (Isaiah 55:8–9 NIV). Although His reasons may elude us and His methods may surprise us, God always fulfills His promises. As the apostle Paul said, "For the foolishness of God is wiser than human wisdom, and the weakness of God is stronger than human strength" (1 Corinthians 1:25 NIV).

We can always have absolute confidence in God to do what He says He will do. We can trust Him to come through because God is faithful. This is based on His character as God:

> God is not a man, so he does not lie.
> He is not human, so he does not change his mind.
> Has he ever spoken and failed to act?
> Has he ever promised and not carried it through? (Numbers 23:19 NLT)

It is contrary to God's divine nature to lie or to make an empty promise. God is not only a promise-giver, He is also a promise keeper. He is rock-solid and consistent when it comes to keeping His Word. And it will be accomplished through His sovereignty.

God is the guarantee of those promises; they are being fulfilled in Him. He wants us to agree that His promises are for us, and they will come to pass.

Remember, God is a promise keeper, not a promise breaker. Whatever He promises, He has the ability and power to bring to pass.

CHAPTER 2

Promises of God

We live in a world of broken promises, don't we? In our society today, it's promises, promises, promises, promises. Governments make promises and break them. Nations make promises and break them. Advertisers make promises and break them. Politicians make promises and break them. Preachers make promises and break them. Husbands, wives, brothers, sisters, moms, dads, uncles, aunts, friends, enemies—everybody makes promises, and everybody breaks them. From relational pain to outlandish political promises to over-the-top ads for fast food, many of us have become skeptical whenever we hear someone make a claim that appears too good to be true. But in a world of broken promises, there is one who never breaks them—never. That is Jesus Christ. God can be counted on.

Let's contemplate the distinctions between God's promises and those of mere humans. Numbers 23:19 (KJV) says, "God is not a man, that he should lie ... hath he said, and shall he not do it? or hath he spoken, and shall he not make it good?"

Why is it impossible for God to lie, and what does that mean for us? First, we must understand that God cannot lie.

His nature is perfect. He has no desire to deceive anyone. He never feels threatened or pressured. If God cannot lie, then His Word is truth. Therefore we have hope.

We humans are weak-willed. Sometimes, out of fear, we make impulsive promises, even though we know we cannot keep them. Keeping promises is considered a measure of one's worth—we prize being "as good as our word." Yet, as humans, we sometimes struggle to keep some of our promises. Other times, it is impossible for us to keep promises because we are sinners and are nothing like God. Ecclesiastes 5:5 (NLV) says, "It is better not to promise anything than to promise something and not do it." This scripture is for believers, not for God. God is faithful in keeping His promises because He is holy and perfect, unlike us. Jesus explains, "Heaven and earth shall pass away, but my words shall not pass away" (Matthew 24:35 KJV).

> A command must be obeyed;
> a promise must be believed.

A promise is the assurance that God gives to His people so they can walk by faith while they wait for Him to work. A promise from God is not a command. A command from God is something we should do; a promise from God is something God will do. A command must be obeyed; a promise must be believed. When God gives a command, He says, "You will." When God gives a promise, He says, "I will." God's entire communication with us can be put into two words: "I promise." We don't have to worry about whether He will make good on what He has promised, because He never overpromises and He never underdelivers.

God's promises are many, running from Genesis to Revelation. These promises reflect God's character. These promises are made by God Himself and therefore will be kept. Aren't you glad that salvation has nothing to do with our promises to God but rather with His promises to us?

As believers, we are heirs of God. But we cannot come into the inheritance without Christ. The promises of God are not without Christ but in Him. One of the reasons why nothing is impossible for God is because God's promises are grounded in Christ. God makes us promises and then waits to see if we shall remain in Him: "Therefore the LORD will wait, that He may be gracious to you; and therefore, He will be exalted, that He may have mercy on you. For the LORD is a God of justice; blessed are all those who wait for Him" (Isaiah 30:18 NKJV).

We must base personal relationship with Jesus on the blood Jesus shed for us, knowing His promises are true, as evidenced by the miraculous changes that a person undergoes when they believe on the Lord Jesus Christ for salvation. We know that Jesus sacrificed His life on the cross of Calvary so that our sins can be forgiven. But He also allowed Himself to be crucified so that the promises of His heavenly Father would be willed to all who believe in Him for salvation. The death and subsequent resurrection and ascension of Jesus Christ legally put all the promises of the Father into our possession. The very word "testament" in the Bible refers to promises. When someone dies, we speak of a last will and testament. Whatever is promised in that last will becomes the legal possession of those who are named in the will.

The same is true with the promises of God. The promises of God are legally willed to all who believe in the sacrificial death and glorious resurrection of Jesus Christ. The epistle to the Hebrews makes that abundantly clear: "In the case of a will, it is necessary to prove the death of the one who made it, because a will is only enforced when somebody has died" (Hebrews 9:16–17 NIV).

The Lord makes promises because He loves us unconditionally and wants to give us guidance, provision, and protection. He reveals Himself in ways that display His awesome wisdom, power, and grace. There's nothing we can do to deserve His promises. It's our responsibility to simply believe and depend upon Him to fulfill them all.

The Word is full of promises that we can take to the bank, day after day, because His character is flawless and He never fails. When we struggle, we can go to the Word, standing on those promises, quoting them back to Him, knowing He bends down to hear our prayers and delights in giving us the deepest desires of our hearts. Once we've known Him a while and felt His ongoing moves in our lives, we can shout from the rooftops of His faithfulness and tender mercies.

But if that's so, why are so many faithful believers living as if these things are *not* so? Scripture talks about hope deferred making the heart grow sick. If we look around us, so many people—perhaps even we ourselves—are looking at those promises and wondering what happened. Why do they (or we) have an endless list of requests that have been prayed over for years and yet have never become manifest?

The interesting thing about a promise is the power it has to change us long before any of the promise is realized. Because a promise gives a believer something to look forward to, to hope for, and to anticipate, it holds great power in the present, even if it is not realized until much later. God uses promises in much the same way: to change us in the present, to give us hope during despair, to anticipate something greater when we have little to base any joy on in the moment. God's promises also have the power to keep us moving in the right direction against tremendous odds.

"For all the promises of God in him are yea, and in him Amen, unto the glory of God by us" (2 Corinthians 1:20 KJV). Notice the apostle's words, "For all the promises of God in him are yea." These promises were all made according to the purpose of His will. We sometimes read or hear or speak of the promises written in God's Word, but do not give them as much credit as if they were the promises of a friend. If we value them more, we should believe them better.

"All the promises," the Old Testament ones as well as those in the New Testament, are sure and steadfast. "All the promises" have been fulfilled. Unfortunately, very few of us believe and access His promises. The Bible contains thousands of great and precious promises that God wants to fulfill in your life (2 Peter 1:4).

> God has set His seal to every divine promise and certifies it with His yea and amen.

"All the promises" in Christ are yea and amen. "Amen" means "so be it, it's already done." In Him, "yea" means the promises are certain. And in Him, "amen" means they are accomplished. If we are going to say yea and amen to God's promises, we need to mean it. We need to agree that God is faithful to do as He said He would do. The stability of the promises in Christ is established. God has set His seal to every divine promise and certifies it with His yea and amen.

God is the great Promiser, the mighty Promiser, and He puts His promises out there for anyone who will receive them. God has equipped us with everything we need to live a godly life. These resources come through God's many promises. Choosing to live obediently gives us the right and privilege to claim His promises. But if we're rebellious and living according to our own desires, we've positioned ourselves outside His will and made His promises ineffective.

Some of God's promises are unconditional, such as God's promise to Abraham: "I will make you into a great nation, and I will bless you; I will make your name great, and you will be a blessing. I will bless those who bless you, and whoever curses you I will curse; and all peoples on earth will be blessed through you" (Genesis 12:2–3 NIV). There was nothing Abraham had to do to receive this promise. It wasn't conditional upon Abraham's response. God just said, "This is what I'm going to do for you."

Some of God's promises are conditional—they require a response for their fulfillment. "Peter replied, 'Repent and be baptized, every one of you, in the name of Jesus Christ for the forgiveness of your sins. And you will receive the gift of the Holy Spirit'" (Acts 2:38 NIV). According to Peter, in order to receive the indwelling presence of the Holy Spirit in their lives, his listeners needed to respond by repenting of their sins and being baptized.

Some of God's promises are limited to certain people and others are universal. The majority of God's promises are made to everyone.

God has a perfect credit score. Even in this world of broken contracts and violated vows, you can still completely trust God's promises. When God says something, it never fails. That's why my goal is to encourage you to read your Bible more, to help you believe in and take advantage of the wonderful array of promises found throughout His Word. We may fail to come through on our promises, but that is never the case with the Lord. His promises never fail. And that is true for every promise that He has made.

CHAPTER 3

Promise and Fulfillment

The word "promise" appears more than one hundred times in the Bible. There are many implied promises. There are promises of man to woman, and woman to man. And there are promises of man to God and God to man. In Isaiah 55:11, God makes it clear that when His Word goes out from His mouth, it will not return to Him empty. It will accomplish what He desires and achieve the purpose for which He sent it. This gives us the assurance that God will always keep His Word. The promises He gives you and the words He speaks over your life will come to pass. God's promises will always bear fruit in your life.

A fulfilled promise can bring joy, life, trust, and even strength into a relationship. For this very reason, I trust the promises of God. His are more certain—and therefore more powerful—than any promise made by any mortal being. We can rely on God's promises not because they are enforceable in a court of law or through social or moral pressure, but because God is God. God is the Being who, Scripture tells us, "lieth not, but fulfilleth all his words" (Number 23:19 KJV).

A promise is only as good as the integrity of the person making it, their worth (in terms of financial backing), or their authority to execute its fulfillment. When you have the promise, you need someone with the power to fulfill the promise.

> There is space and time between promise and fulfillment.

There is space and time between promise and fulfillment. This is a time for preparation. It is a time when we are pressed like clay in the hands of God. It is a place of feeling isolated, even abandoned. You feel like the days passing by are taking you no closer to your destiny and the fulfillment of your prophetic promises. What do you do when you are not sure what God is up to in your life? This is a common experience, and it can be disorienting if we do not understand what God is doing or how to respond to it. Some people call it "the wilderness," and for good reason. Like Joseph in Egypt, the Israelites on their way to the Promised Land, David in exile, and many other figures in Scripture, we are amid a process between the promise and fulfillment.

In the space between, we learn to dream God's dreams. We discover God as our source in every situation. We learn how to respond to temptation, injustice, and pain. We not only endure obstacles and storms, but we also become victorious in them and rise above them. In the wilderness, we learn to recognize divine invitation and wage war with the promises God has given to us. Regardless of what we are going through, in the wilderness we learn to find our delight in God alone.

The fulfillment of His promises may require us to do something that appears contradictory (Genesis 22:1–5). Although the Lord had clearly said the world would be blessed through Isaac, He tested Abraham's faith by telling him to sacrifice his beloved son. Abraham obeyed, and the Lord intervened and provided a ram instead. Whenever God tests us, we should follow Abraham's example and live by faith and obedience, not by emotions and human reasoning.

The fulfillment of the Lord's promises may seem impossible from our perspective (Genesis 17:16–19). When God told Abraham that Sarah would bear a son when she was ninety, it seemed so impossible that Abraham laughed. This is why we should not underestimate the Lord. If we are obedient when He challenges us with something that seems impossible, He will keep His Word and pour out more amazing blessings than we can even imagine.

The fulfillment of the Lord's promises may include the surrender of something very dear to us (Genesis 22:2). Isaac was Abraham's treasured child, yet Abraham was willing to surrender him to God. We must each ask ourselves if there's anything so dear to us that we are unwilling to give it to the Lord. At some point, He may bring us to a pivotal moment when His purpose rests on a single decision. Even if the choice is costly, we must do what God asks and let go of anything we value more than Him. When we do, God will do His part by fulfilling the promise.

When you are living between the promise and the fulfillment, you must be able to see past circumstances and into God's reality. This ability is powerful! I know it is hard sometimes to accept a promise when your reality reflects the opposite of what has been spoken over your life. But you must believe that the promise will come to pass.

God's promise to Abraham was not merely the promise of a son. God also promised to make Abraham a "great nation" (Genesis 12:2, 15:5, 17:5–6). The son was just the beginning. Abraham was one hundred and sixty years old when his grandsons Jacob and Esau were born. The "great nation" was still one seed, Jacob. It was not in Abraham's lifetime that the promise of a great nation was fulfilled.

God also promised Abraham a great land that his "seed" would possess. This was the land of Canaan (Genesis 12:5–7, 13:14–15), the boundaries of which were more fully defined in Genesis 15:18–21. At the time of Sarah's death, the land of Canaan was possessed by the Canaanites (Genesis 12:6). Abraham did not own any part of the Promised Land. Abraham had to buy a small parcel of ground as a burial site for his family (Genesis 23:1–20).

> If we really want all that God has for us,
> then we must give all we have to Him!

If we expect God to bless us, then we must comply with His divine requirements. It is no use going our own way and then complaining that God is not blessing us! There must be obedience to the revealed Word of God. That way ensures His blessing.

God takes us forward step by step. When we are obedient to what He has shown us, then He will show us the next step to take. This is a basic principle in the path of blessing. If we really want all that God has for us, then we must give all we have to Him! This is total abandonment of self to God's revealed will for our lives—following God when He shows us the way forward and obeying His voice when He speaks to us, without any reservation at all!

Never lose the joy of your promise. "For the vision is yet for an appointed time ... though it tarry, wait for it; because it will surely come" (Habakkuk 2:3). Remember, the purpose of the promises is that God may be glorified.

Waiting on God is painful. The pain of waiting on the promises of God involves time passing by while nothing is happening—or so it seems. Fear, anxiety, and impatience always show up when promises seem stagnant. I've discovered that life is scary when you have promises and no answers. Unfortunately, most people give up before stepping into the promise. To counteract these feelings, you must carry expectancy, believing that something is going to happen in due time.

We don't always see what God is doing in our lives. We

see problems really well, but we don't necessarily see God moving us in the direction of the promise. During this time, we have a lot of questions but not a lot of solid answers. We need something to help us through those tough times when it looks like God's promises are in doubt.

I grew up believing in the promises of God. I remember the songs my mother sang in church: "Every promise in the Bible is mine; every verse, every chapter, every line."[1] I learned that the promises of God are unfailing, and they are upheld by His oath. Since God had no one greater than Himself, He swore by Himself. He based His oath on His own great name, guaranteeing He would accomplish His purpose and execute His promises.

Can you hold on to what God has said, even when the promises don't appear to be coming true?

---

[1] Arranged by Pearl Spencer Smith, "Every Promise in the Book Is Mine," *Yes, Lord! Church of God in Christ Hymnal* (Memphis: Church of Christ Publishing House, 1982), https://hymnary.org/text/every_promise_in_the_book#pagescans.

CHAPTER 4

Promise Power

God's promises are obligations that He imposes upon Himself. He has promised, and He will do it. Why? God has power. He has the power to execute His promises. When we speak of God being all-powerful, we often use the word "omnipotent." According to Vocabulary.com, this word comes from the Latin words *omnis*, which means "all," and *potens*, which means "power." If you prefer a simpler definition, just think of these three words: "God is able." That's what omnipotence means.

Scripture affirms God's omnipotence by saying that God does whatever He is pleased to do (Psalm 115:3; Isaiah 55:11; Jeremiah 32:17). Nothing is too hard for Him (Genesis 18:14). His Word is never void of power, so when He speaks, everything in creation obeys Him (Isaiah 55:11). His Word always prevails, and we can trust that His prophecies always happen (Deuteronomy 18:21–22).

God is matchless in power and unconquerable. He not only has ultimate power over all things, but He is also the Source of all power. God can do anything that can be done. He can do anything that is possible, and God can do what humans deem impossible. God can accomplish whatever He pleases. No matter what you're facing right now, God has the power to deliver you. Nothing is too hard *or* too complicated for His power to solve. No battle is too strong for His power to conquer. No need is too great for His power to supply. No burden is so heavy that His power cannot lift it. No prayer is too impossible for His power to answer.

If you search Scripture, you will find that the Bible has a lot to say about the power of God. In the Old Testament, one of the Hebrew names of the living God is Abir, which means "the mighty One" or "to be strong."[2] In the New Testament, the Hebrew name for God is Pantokrator, which means "the all-powerful One; all-ruling."[3] God is more powerful than nature and stronger than the sea. He is firm in His strength. It was His power that set the stars and galaxies in place. It was His ability that determined the boundaries for land and sea. God spoke and it came to be. He commanded and everything stood firm (Psalms 33:4).

> The awesomeness of God is that He is not controlled by power, He *is* power.

The awesomeness of God is that He is not controlled by power, He *is* power. There is no power in the world greater than Him. That's why He is called El Shaddai, which

---

[2] https://www.abarim-publications.com/Meaning/Abir.html
[3] https://hermeneutics.stackexchange.com/questions/2616/what-does-pantokrator-mean

means "the almighty God" or "the all-sufficient One."[4] His power is infinite, which means unlimited. His power is eternal, which means it will never go out of business. The power of God cannot be confined or contained, restrained or restricted, prohibited or prevented by anything or anybody. His power cannot be measured, for it proceeds beyond boundaries. There is no deficiency or defect in His power. There is no lack or shortage of His power. He has no power failures, no power shortages, and no power outages. Every time you flip the switch, God's power is right there.

God's promised power is amazing. He is the power source and the power supply. His power is manifested strength. It is demonstrated authority. It's massive. It's explosive. It's effectual and wonderworking. God's power is like Himself, self-existent and self-sustained. It is not acquired from someone. It does not depend upon any other authority outside of Himself. The domain of His power and strength lies within Him.

Clearly the Bible affirms God's power. "His power is vast" (Job 9:4). The Lord is "strong and mighty" (Psalm 24:8). Out of His "great power and mighty strength," God brought forth the universe (Isaiah 40:26). Don't these passages indicate there is no limit to God's power? Absolutely.

Many Christians believe that because God is omnipotent, He can do anything. They are correct. All of God's promises

---

[4] Becky Harling, "What Is the Significance of El Shaddai?" *Crosswalk*, updated July 27, 2021, https://www.crosswalk.com/faith/bible-study/what-is-the-significance-of-el-shaddai.html.

have power. They extend God's lifeline of hope. He offers them before we ever need them. They lift you up when things look bleak. They are answers to our life's needs. And they are solutions to our problems—current and future ones.

> God's power is strong. It is not intimidated by our circumstances or threatened by our trouble.

God's power is strong. It is not intimidated by our circumstances or threatened by our trouble. His power breaks down barriers and walls and makes possible what was impossible! His power can get us through bad times, broke times, and hard times.

When we understand that God is omnipotent, our chaotic world doesn't seem quite so scary. All we must do is rely on His power, which holds the whole ocean in His hand and created the land on which we stand and walk. As believers, we can put our trust in Him and the promises He has given to us in His Word.

Nothing is impossible with God. *Nothing.* Not even *that* thing. *Your* thing. God has the power to fulfill every promise spoken over your life. He has the power to do all that is consistent with His nature. He will not go back on His Word. He loves to display His power through the lives of His people. God has *promise* power.

CHAPTER 5

Process to the Promise

Before God walks you into the promise, He walks you through the process. A promise from God always requires a process. So often, we want the promise, but we do not want to go through God's process to get us there. God is more interested in the journey than the destination. It is through the process that God fulfills His promise.

A process is a series of actions or steps taken to achieve a particular goal. All throughout the Bible are people who received a promise from God but still had to endure the process to receive it. Sarah and Abraham (Genesis 18–21), the children of Israel (Exodus 2:23; Joshua 24), David (1 Samuel 16:12; 2 Samuel 8:15) Mary and Martha (John 11), and even Jesus had to go through a process before the promises of God were fulfilled in their lives. The devil offered Jesus the world, but Jesus knew no matter how good it might sound, the devil could never offer the promises of God.

Very rarely do we receive a promise and not have to experience a process associated with it. The process is designed to cause us to trust God as He orders our steps toward the promise. Much as we would like instant results—instant food, instant delivery, instant feedback—God does not work with "instant." God works with process. He works in steps toward a transformation, a journey, or a destination. Scripture tells us that the steps of a man are ordered by the Lord (Psalm 37:23), which means that God works in us step by step and not instantly. We must learn to embrace the process that leads to what He promised.

There are times when God puts things in our hearts— dreams, aspirations, goals—and gives them to us right away. There are other times when God puts things in our hearts and then makes us wait. He may have promised you a new home, a new job, or a new business, but you still have a process that you must go through to realize those things. God could give us a free pass and allow us to skip the process, but what would we really gain from that? Can we see how strong we are if our strength and faith are never tested?

> God created the process to make
> the promise even better.

God created the process to make the promise even better. God's process is a time of testing, like the testing of your faith or your obedience. He teaches us things. He grows our character, our faith, and our ability to do what we feel called to do. God's process involves breaking—not the breaking of us, but the breaking of things *in* us, like a prideful spirit or a stubborn mindset. God's process involves shaping, a molding of our new person, a new creation in Christ. This could be the development of a new mindset or a shaping of our relationships.

Finally, God's process involves gratitude. We should never forget how blessed we are. Sometimes we need to go through a process of remembering and developing gratitude and thanksgiving in our hearts.

Often, the devil is more aware than we are of how close we are to a major breakthrough. Right now, many Christians are on the verge of seeing their greatest hopes and desires spring forth after years of standing in faith. The enemy would love to short-circuit this by bringing compromise into the process. Once the devil realizes he cannot budge us from believing in the fulfillment of all God has for us, he tries to entice us to accept the promise in a way that perverts it and nullifies it.

One of the secrets to receiving from God is perseverance. Perseverance is important. "Perseverance" means the continued effort to do or achieve something, even when it is difficult or takes a long time. The popular colloquial phrases describing it include "Keep on keeping on," "Hang in there," "Put up with it," and "Don't quit." Its synonyms are "determination," "endurance," "tenacity," "plodding," "stamina," and "backbone."

When the word "endurance" is used in the Bible, it means "to abide under," "to bear up courageously," and "to tarry or wait." [5]We see an example of this in the life of Job.

---

[5] http://glorybooks.org/greek-word-endurance-hypomone/

Job endured immense suffering, losing his wealth, health, and family. Despite it all, he remained faithful and patient and received twice as much in the end. If you can wait long enough on God, you can get whatever you need from Him.

Do you know how long it took Hannah to have the child of promise? What about Elizabeth, the mother of John the Baptist? Be determined like Jacob and say to God, "I will not let you go until you have fulfilled all your promises to me" (Genesis 32:26).

Most of us have become conditioned to a fast-paced life. From daily activities to our needs and wants, we want it all now. Waiting, therefore, is hard. The process can be long, but learn to love your process. Thank God for the work He is doing in your life, even if you don't understand what He is doing. Just know that God has something incredible planned for you, and your process will lead you to the promise.

So how are you embracing God's process? Is God being glorified through it? Are you making His name great during your journey to the promise He has spoken over your life? Are you exercising your faith? Faith is what keeps us going until we see God do what He has promised. Faith causes us to say, "I may not have seen it yet, but if God promised it, I am sure I will!"

I believe the Lord is saying in this hour that for each of us to truly come into our destiny, we must not only embrace His promises, but we must also embrace His process. What we do is important, and the way we do it is just as important.

Many of us have fought a good fight of faith for a long time. This is not the time to let the devil come, in a moment of weakness or fatigue, and tempt you into accepting something that looks like the promise you have been believing for. Stand strong. You are closer than you can imagine to walking in the fulfillment of all you have hoped, prayed, and believed for.

My friend, if you settle in your mind that you *will* go through the process that God will use to bring about His promises, it will strengthen your faith.

CHAPTER 6

Preparation for the Promise

Preparation must come before the promise. Preparation will determine if we are ready for the promise. Successes and big opportunities don't just happen, even in God's economy. They come to those who are prepared. If you shortcut the process, you short-circuit the product, which is you.

The place of adequate preparation is one of immense importance. When you have an unclouded vision of what God wants you to achieve in life, you begin preparing yourself to accomplish those goals. By preparing yourself, you are in a position to take advantage of countless opportunities that come into your path.

Preparation is an act of anticipation, meaning that we prepare because we expect something good and beneficial to manifest in our lives. Preparing for opportunities also means that you are consistently taking action in your life to work toward your goals.

> The problem is God does not hate delays. He uses them frequently on our journey to prepare us for the future.

Waiting is the hardest part. I hate delays. I do everything I can to avoid them. I stay away from certain streets and the freeway during high-traffic hours in Los Angeles because I hate delays. The problem is God does not hate delays. He uses them frequently on our journey to prepare us for the future. A delay is the gap between the moment when God awakens dreams, speaks promises, or calls you to an assignment, and the moment when it comes to pass. The way we respond to delay plays a critical role in our preparation for the promise.

God is preparing you today for the promise that will come tomorrow. Because we don't always understand God's ways, we may think we are ready for anything. We've been reading, praying, fasting, listening to good teaching, and going to church. What else do we have to do? We must believe that God knows what He is doing while we go through the preparation process.

The enemy wants us to believe that God is a liar, that there is no chance that His promises—His Word—will come to pass. However, we must believe that when God promises something, it will happen. All you have to do is wait, believe, and stay in His will. You cannot rush God. Be patient.

When God says something about Himself in His Word, it is assured to be true, to have been true, and to always be true. When He describes Himself, it is a promise. When He speaks of His deeds, it is a promise. When He declares His love or protection or presence, it is a promise. And when He says He will keep His promises, it is a promise.

Promises are intended to strengthen your walk. They are intended to keep you looking unto Jesus. Promises are meant to bring joy, hope, and a testimony. But waiting is painful. Replace your pain with praise. Don't be fixated on what you feel or think, but on what you believe. Rather than pleading with God to speed up the promise, view waiting as a gift. Give God praise for the waiting room.

It is easy to praise God when we receive the promise. The true test is when we can praise God while waiting on Him. Praising God helps us to keep our eyes on Him and look forward to receiving the promise. Praising God in the waiting room is one of the most beautiful lessons I've learned on this journey. When I look back on my journey, I see God's hand in each moment.

Perhaps you feel that the dream God planted in your heart will never come to pass. Don't stress about your lack of open doors. Do what God gives you to do now with excellence, and you'll be ready for the bigger opportunity when He brings it to you. You may be saying, "I have been waiting too long. If I had to wait one year, I could handle it, but I have been waiting five, ten, twenty years!" Let me remind you that God's timing is a mystery. Some of the greatest figures in the Bible—Abraham, Joseph, Moses, David—had to wait for many years for God's promises. Everything that happened in the meantime was used to prepare them, inwardly as well as outwardly. Then, when they reached their promise, they were blessed beyond measure.

Promises are great! We get very excited when we hear God speak specifically to us about a particular thing. It always feels good that God knows you personally and has great plans for your life. But I've found that promises—a great gift from God—can turn into a source of distress when it appears that it is taking forever for the promise to come to pass. The fact is promises do not always manifest immediately. Waiting can be painful. Waiting can be disheartening, especially when it's longer than expected.

Have you ever asked God to make something happen in your life, and it appears as if that thing won't come to pass? During this time, the enemy may make you feel unhappy and hopeless. It is not because God's promises failed you or because God abandoned you, but because the enemy's job is to make you feel hopeless. When waiting takes too long, it hurts.

God will cause us to wait on Him, and that too will be painful. There is a lot of pain in waiting upon God to act. The trials and tests He sends us will build patient submission and won't be easy ones. He will send big ones because of the stronghold impatience has upon us.

Waiting is something we rarely do anymore. So why would we be patient? Why would we be willing to accept God's timing? Even not getting the things we want is rarer than ever, because we can "have it our way"! However, what we want is not always what we *need*.

> We must always remember that the enemy
> wants to get us out of alignment with the Lord.

We must always remember that the enemy wants to get us out of alignment with the Lord. One of the ways the enemy tries to accomplish this is by causing us to become impatient, to distrust the promises of God, or to abandon them too early. We need to be patient and trust in God's promises. The way to do that is to fix our eyes on God. If we start comparing the time we've spent waiting for a promise with the time others appear to have spent waiting, we will be terribly frustrated. God has a unique design for each of our lives. And because He is God, our time of preparation and our season of growth will be unlike those of anyone else.

There is a frequent pattern to the process:

- God gives a prophetic promise to His people, but then time passes by.
- There is weakness, there is waiting, and there are trials.

A preparing season is also a teaching season. We may need training, building, organizing, recruiting, or hiring, but there will be something that we need to do. While we know what we want, God knows what we need, how much we need it, and when we should receive it. Even though the promise God gave you is for a future time, faith and anticipation will cause you to prepare now.

What is God preparing you for? Could your waiting season mean that God is preparing you for the things you don't even know are coming? Just know that God is preparing you today for what He wants to do through you in the future.

If you reach your destination without trials, you will feel as if you have done it through your own strength, not God's.

CHAPTER 7

God's Promise to One Man

Not every promise in the Bible applies to every person in the world. Some promises are given to particular people in a certain time and place. For instance, when God told Abraham and Sarah they would have a son, this was His commitment specifically to them, not to anyone else (Genesis 17:15–16). Second, it's important to realize some promises are conditional. Consider the Bible verse that says, "Delight yourself in the Lord; and He will give you the desires of your heart" (Psalm 37:4). This isn't an open-ended guarantee that God will give you whatever you want. There's a qualification: delighting in the Lord and desiring what He wants.

Even though some of God's promises have restrictions, there are many in the New Testament that apply to all believers. God promises to work all things together for our good (Romans 8:28), to be with us forever (Hebrews 13:5), and to give us an eternal inheritance in heaven (1 Peter 1:3–5). We can claim these with full assurance because Scripture explicitly tells us they're God's will.

But let's get back to Abraham.

In the book of Genesis, we see many of examples of God making promises to Abraham and fulfilling them. Abraham was once called Abram. He was an idol worshipper. He lived with his father and other relatives in a place called Haran. God called Abram to worship and serve Him. He instructed Abram to leave his country, his relatives, and his father's house and go to the land of Canaan. Abraham was seventy-five years old when God called him for his kingdom purpose.

God made several promises to Abraham:

- I will make of you the father of a great nation.
- I will bless you and make your name great.
- I will bless those who bless you and curse them who curse you.
- In you all the families of the earth shall be blessed.
- I will give your descendants the land of Canaan.

"Leave your native country, your relatives, and your father's family, and go to the land that I will show you. I will make you into a great nation … All the families on earth will be blessed through you" (Genesis 12:1–3). When Abraham heard God's call, he believed what God promised, and he obeyed. He took his wife, his nephew Lot, his servants, and all his possessions and left Haran to go the land of Canaan.

Most of the time God's promise to Abraham is viewed in relationship to Israel, and rightfully so. But I want to add another thought to this promise, because this promise has a greater reach than just Israel.

Abram heard the promise of God and believed the Lord. God had already given Abram major promises in Genesis 12. Abram had worshipped the Lord at various altars he had built in Genesis 12–13. The Lord had shown Abram the land He would give to him and his descendants in Genesis 13. And God had infused Abram with power to fight and given him the Melchizedekian blessing in Genesis 14. Abram believed the Lord and the Lord counted it to Abram as righteousness. The apostle James cites this verse and claims that because of his faith Abraham became the "friend of God" (James 2:23).

Abram's believed God's promises. God loved this faith and counted it to Abram as righteousness. Righteousness is thus reckoned by God to the one who believes.

God fulfilled all the promises He made to Abraham through Jacob. The Bible says that while Jacob slept, he dreamed there was a ladder that reached heaven from the ground. He saw God's angels climbing up and down the ladder. Then he saw God standing above the ladder and saying, "I am the Lord, the God of Abraham your father and the God of Isaac. I will give to you and your descendants the land you are lying down on" (Genesis28:13). God repeated the promise He had made to Abraham. He promised to be with Jacob and to bring him back to the land of Canaan.

The story of the birth of Isaac was God's fulfillment of His promise to Abraham. Isaac became the father of Jacob, who later become the father of the twelve tribes of Israel.

The blessing you and I receive is God's fulfillment of His promise to one man, Abraham.

Abraham is the father of faith. He lived in between the promise and the fulfillment. God reassured him of the future He'd planned for Abraham, and Abraham believed God.

> God takes from His best and shares it with us.

Abraham's story is not that different from ours. God's promise didn't make sense based on Abraham's circumstances, just like ours don't make sense based on our circumstances. Promises are usually made when the situation doesn't match what God is telling you. That is the beauty of God's promises: they don't have to make sense. God is not limited by your circumstances. He is able to move in spite of them, which is exactly what He did with Abraham.

God blessed Abraham so that Abraham could bless others. This truth is not just for Abraham; it is true for you and me as well. When God blesses, He never intends for the blessing to be kept to ourselves. That goes against God's character. God takes from His best and shares it with us. He expects us to do the same. Everything God gives us may be for our enjoyment, but it is not for our *exclusive* enjoyment. God blessed Abraham so he could be a blessing. God blesses you for the same reason. Whatever the degree to which God has blessed us, we should in turn bless others.

If God has given you great wisdom and knowledge, bless others with it. If He has given you artistic and creative ability, bless others with it. If He has given you leadership and business acumen, bless others with it. Whether God has given you much or little you should bless others with it.

The greatest offspring that came from Abraham's lineage was Jesus Christ. Therefore, this blessing and cursing do not just apply to the way we treat Israel. They apply to the way we treat Jesus.

CHAPTER 8

Promises Require Commitment

A promise requires at least two parties who are willing to commit to the process. When God asked Abraham to leave behind everyone and everything that was familiar and follow Him to a place Abraham knew nothing about, that was a big ask! It required some serious commitment on Abraham's part. But then, think about God's end of the bargain: "I will make you a great nation … every human being will be blessed because of you" (Genesis 12:2-3)! That was big too! Especially since Abraham was seventy-five years old, Sarah was sixty, and they had never had children.

Abraham and Sarah committed to the process and relocated to a faraway land, where they prospered and increased. It was difficult to leave the support and security of his home country, but Abraham trusted God unconditionally. This was a massive leap of faith!

Like Abraham, Jesus wants us to be totally committed to following Him, no matter how difficult the challenge may be. Jesus wants followers who trust Him enough to say, "I won't stay in the comfort of what's familiar. I trust You and will follow You in whatever cross You have shaped and chosen for me to carry."

Most of God's promises are conditional. He says, "If you will do this, then I will do that." We have no right to claim the promise unless we first meet the condition He puts forth.

Our God of promise desires for us to listen to His voice and obey. It's one thing to believe what He says is true. It's another thing to obey what He says. When we obey His Word and honor our commitments to Him, we will receive all that He has promised us.

It should be the goal of each born-again believer to live a life that is totally committed to God. We have a God who honors His commitments, keeps His promises, and fulfills His Word.

However, when we choose to commit ourselves to following Him, we truly don't know where He will lead us or what experiences we may have. All we know is that the Person we are following is trustworthy and that He will lead us on the right road.

> God wants you to be committed to Him so that the world may know He is important to you.

Real commitment involves resolution, a pledge, a promise, devotion, a commission, and determination. One of the best ways of showing our reverence to God is through our commitment. God wants you to be committed to Him so that the world may know He is important to you. In other words, if you honor Him, He will honor you. If you sow to God, He will allow you to reap from Him. This is too important for us to miss.

God has always demanded a total commitment from His children. In the Old Testament, He demanded total commitment from the Israelites. "Hear, O Israel: The LORD our God, the LORD is one! You shall love the LORD your God with all your heart, with all your soul, and with all your strength" (Deuteronomy 6:4–5 NKJV). But the children of Israel often failed in this regard and served other gods.

I have discovered on this Christian journey that the enemy loves to direct our attention away from God. He uses people and situations to distract us from living a committed lifestyle unto God. This can be quickly changed by repenting, rebuking the enemy, and putting our focus right back on the Lord. We are just like the Israelites in this.

Commitment, in the context of this chapter, means loyalty, devotion, or dedication to God. God says, "You shall have no other gods before Me" (Exodus 20:3 NKJV). He says there is no God besides Him (Deuteronomy 32:39; Isaiah 44:8, 45:5, 21). God wants His children to have undivided loyalty to Him. He wants them to be totally committed to Him. God wants you to earnestly obey His Word, love Him, and serve Him with all your heart and with all your soul (Deuteronomy 11:13).

We are told to commit our ways to the Lord in everything we do. David told us to trust in God and also explained why

(Psalm 37). When we trust God, we remain confident that following Him will lead to God's and our own satisfaction. Proverbs says, "Commit to the Lord whatever you do, and he will establish your plans" (16:3 NIV). Sadly, many men and women give lip service to this well-known verse. They think it means they can say the words of the verse and then do their own thing. This is not what is meant. Satan tricks many with this deception. God is the One who will establish you and your plans. If something isn't working, it isn't God, because what God wants to work will work. Sadly, much energy is wasted when Christians think it is their job to "establish" their plans. Commit all to Him and live according to His ways. There will be peace, joy, contentment, and abundance.

I strongly believe your commitment shows your values, shapes your life, and determines your destiny. When dedicating your works to God, strive to align your desires and plans with His greater purpose. You can achieve this by submitting your goals to His divine wisdom. By doing so, you open yourself up to receiving blessings from God beyond your expectations.

It's not wrong to express your personal desires and wishes before God. The key is to align them with His divine intentions. In fact, the Bible mentions in Psalm 37:4 that He will grant you the desires of your heart. Avoid letting your desires obstruct God's destined path for you. Instead, embrace His divine plan and release your grip on control.

When we exclude God from our plans,
we demonstrate that we are not
truly seeking His will.

Regrettably, we often make decisions without first seeking God's approval, unintentionally reducing His role to that of a mere rubber stamp. When we exclude God from our plans, we demonstrate that we are not truly seeking His will.

To be fully committed is to be daily submitted. Always give yourselves fully to the work of the Lord. Every day, we need to come before God and submit our will to His. We need to submit our desires, our goals, and our plans to His desires, His goals, and His plans.

How about you? How far would you be willing to go just on someone's word? How big of a promise would you dare commit to? When it comes to getting into agreement with God regarding His promises, those are the issues you need to resolve. Rest assured God will keep His Word; He just needs your commitment to move forward.

CHAPTER 9

Promise and Pain

There is pain in promise, but we must rise above it. This pain does not come from God but from the evil one. The enemy specializes in making good things look bad. He makes righteous people subjects of ridicule.

Just because God has given you a promise does not mean that everything will go smoothly. There will be challenges along the way. But a promise that is from God will always stand the test of time.

You might have some indications about the future as you move through your seasons. When things happen unexpectedly and blessings start flowing in your life, not everybody will be happy for you. When you step into your promise season and new opportunities, it will be extremely exciting, but it can also be painful. To feel pain during moments of blessing does not make you any less spiritual or less faithful. It just means you are human. Yet again, you will be reminded how desperately you need Jesus—in the blessings and in the trials.

Have you ever had moments when a blessing in your life doesn't exactly feel like a blessing? Maybe you're going through a life transition that you know is good, but it still hurts. Maybe it's getting a new home or a brand-new car. Maybe it's packing your car to send your baby off to college. That's a good thing. Leaving home is a natural step in your child's process to becoming an adult, but that doesn't make it easy. Maybe it's a career shift. Your new job is something you've wanted, but the transition feels a bit more painful and terrifying than you dreamed of. It is a blessing, but it doesn't feel like a blessing for you.

> **There are many seasons in life when blessings seem to be wrapped in pain.**

Sometimes there's pain in the blessing. There are many seasons in life when blessings seem to be wrapped in pain. But we can't let the pain rob us of enjoying the promise.

This pain will sometimes come from people—people who are jealous of your blessing. Jealousy cannot stand it when others are doing better. You see this, for example, in one of the stories concerning Isaac. We read how Isaac was able to plant crops and reap a blessing in the land to which he had gone, so much so that the Bible says, "He became rich, and his wealth continued to grow until he became [exceptionally] wealthy" (Genesis 26:13). And that "he had so many flocks and herds and servants that the Philistines envied him. So, all the wells that his father's servants had dug in the time of his father Abraham, the Philistines stopped up, filling them with earth" (Genesis 26:14-33). The Philistines came with their little backhoes, as it were, and they said, "Oh, so you think you're doing well, Mr. Wealthy Isaac? Well, let's show you what this feels like." And they filled up his wells. Why? Because they couldn't stand that he was doing better than they were.

Jealousy is sad at the happiness of others. We see this on display in the parable of the Prodigal Son in Luke 15. You remember the story. The youngest son demanded his inheritance early, left his older brother behind, went off to a distant country, wasted everything his father had given him, made a mess of things, ended up in a pigsty, and finally decided to go home. With a penitent heart, he figured he would serve his father. Instead, his father determined to provide the best of parties for his younger son, as well as a whole new outfit, shoes for his feet, and a ring to wear. The father ordered the servants to kill the fatted calf for a feast.

When the elder brother heard the music and the dancing in his father's house, he refused to go in. Why? He was sad at the happiness of others.

Jealousy makes us hostile toward those who have never harmed us. In the story of Joseph from the Old Testament, you'll remember that when his brothers saw how their father loved Joseph, "they hated him and could not speak a kind word to him" (Genesis 37:4). To be fair, there were extenuating circumstances involved. For example, Jacob showed favoritism toward Joseph, and Joseph didn't know how to keep his dreams to himself. But the point is clear—Joseph hadn't done anything to harm his brothers, yet they hated him. And the reason they hated him was because the seeds of jealousy were deep in their hearts.

Jealousy is not new; it has been around since people began to inhabit the earth. Jealousy is cruel as the grave" and may seek to bring about the ruin of the one whom we envy (Song of Solomon 8:6). Jealousy will rot your bones. It will suffocate you. It will trap you. It will enslave you. Proverbs 14:30 says, "A heart at peace gives life to the body, but jealousy/envy rots the bones." It breeds a destructive, critical spirit. The Bible tells us that jealousy can even make us sick: "A heart at peace gives life to the body, but envy rots the bones" (Proverbs 14:30 NIV).

When God starts blessing you, people will walk away from you, talk about you, and/or try to take you down. And it will hurt. It will be painful. Early in the book of Genesis, Cain was jealous of Abel and murdered him because of it. In 1 Samuel, King Saul was so jealous of David that he continually tried to kill him. At times the jealousy drove him mad. In addition, some of Jesus's twelve disciples were jealous of one another, asking Him which of them was the greatest.

Just remember, when people are jealous of you because God is blessing you, it has nothing to do with you and everything to do with them. Be confident in yourself. Don't allow a jealous person to make you feel unworthy for receiving the promise. Count your blessings and move on.

Everybody is not meant to enjoy your blessings. The psalmist knew this truth when he wrote, "It is good for me that I was afflicted, that I might learn your statutes" (Psalm 119:71). But do not be discouraged. I am sure the psalmist didn't arrive at the point of recognizing the good in his suffering overnight. Neither will we.

CHAPTER 10

It's a Promise, Not a Problem

Between the promise that God gives to you and His provision, He will often send a problem to make you, not kill you. A problem is something to be worked out. It's a demand placed upon us without an apparent solution. It is a matter or situation regarded as unwelcome or harmful and needing to be dealt with and overcome.

As believers, we cannot view a promise as a problem. Our actions demonstrate that we view promises as problems when God is not moving according to our timetable. Instead of recognizing the delay as a blessing, we see it as a problem, especially if the delay is extended. When this happens, disappointment and a sense of betrayal can seep in. The problems that come in your life will either make you wait on God or give up on God.

Promises are supposed to give us hope. They are exciting, something to look forward to and plan for, not to be seen as a problem. When we become discouraged, even give up, we turn a promise into a problem.

Think about this: a problem in our eyes could be a tool in God's view, chiseling away some besetting weight or sin. A problem could be the motivation needed to live better or become involved in something we wouldn't otherwise have done. Are you walking through a problem that seems beyond your capacity to resolve? Trust in God.

> God wants us to see our problems
> as possibilities whenever He has spoken
> a promise over our lives.

God wants us to see our problems as possibilities whenever He has spoken a promise over our lives. Why? God sees problems from a divine viewpoint, which looks at trials, troubles, and tribulations through the eyes of God, through the Word of God, and through the promises of God by the power of the Holy Spirit. According to the Bible, "As for God, his way is perfect" (Psalm 18:30). God knows what is best for us. God uses problems to direct us, to teach us, to strengthen us, and to help us grow. When we begin to see things from this perspective, our problems become smaller and smaller.

God made a promise to Joseph in his dreams when Joseph was about seventeen years old. Joseph was so excited that he bragged about it to his older brothers, mother, and father. Thirteen years and a lot of hardship later, suddenly the promise began to take shape. Overnight he went from being in prison to being the second-in-command of one of the world powers of that day. Seven or eight years later, what he had seen in his dream became reality as his brothers bowed before him.

When Joseph first received the promise, he did not understand God's purpose behind it. He just knew he would be lord over this family. As the youngest of many brothers, he was excited by that idea. But God took him on a journey that gave Joseph the empathy, skills, and wisdom he would need to fulfill the purpose of God when God fulfilled the promise to him. Psalm 105:19 (TPT) says, "God's promise to Joseph purged his character until it was time for his dreams to come true."

God's delay in fulfilling the promise brought on a problem, but the problem had a purpose.

We have all received promises from God. Some are fulfilled quickly; others require patient endurance. But rest assured, God does not forget His promises. Psalm 111:5 says, "He satisfies all who love and trust him, and he keeps every promise he makes." We may not understand how or why, but any delay in the fulfillment of a promise of God has a divine purpose.

How you see the problem *is* the problem. If the truth be told, there are times in our Christian experience when we don't feel like God keeps His promises. There are times when it looks like God has said one thing and the opposite is taking place. When it comes to God's promises, we know He can't lie—but sometimes *you* lie to you, because what

He says and what you are seeing do not match. Sometimes it looks like God is bailing on us.

It's important to understand that there is often a lapse of time between the giving of God's promise and its fulfillment. This time gap occurs because God is getting His promise ready for you and getting you ready for His promise. Don't see this time as problem. There's a purpose and a promise for every problem in life. Let's find the purpose and claim the promises.

CHAPTER 11

The Promise is Controlled by God

As fallible human beings with limited human minds, we often struggle to grasp that there is truly Someone who is perfectly trustworthy in every way and knows us completely. This is who God is. I'm convinced that as believers, it's essential that we understand what it means when we say our God is all-knowing. His knowledge is unlimited. The Bible clearly says that the most vital thing we humans can possess is not just a sense of His character, but the ability to know God personally. I find it stunning to realize that He is not interested in being a dictator or a long-distance potentate. He created us, and He loves us, knowing exactly what makes us tick. He loves our various individual personalities and never intended us to be cookie-cutter followers. In fact, if you recall, He spent hours walking and talking with Adam and Eve in the cool of the day in the garden of Eden (Genesis 3:8). He wouldn't have done that had He not been interested in their thoughts and feelings. He wants to use those differences to reach a big, wide world, where it will require all of our special qualities to win the lost.

Unlike human beings, our God has unlimited, unacquired knowledge and a complete grasp of everything. He has no need to ponder His options, nor does He pace back and forth in confusion to come up with solutions to our problems. Nowhere does He have problem-solving on His to-do list, because He already knows how to handle everything, whether we're aware of it or not. And because He knows us and everything about us so completely, He simply knows what to do, as well as when and how. He knows exactly what to do, just because He is God. Because He is unchanging and eternal, His grasp of the facts is comprehensive. Not only that, but also He is love. He uses His knowledge with our very best interests at heart, knowing the beginning from the end, ever ready to turn every situation around for our good, no matter how bad it looks to us. Nothing ever surprises Him, and nothing ever will. Once we understand these things, we can walk in confidence, knowing He is trustworthy and wants to be our dearest friend and most trustworthy confidante.

God is already aware of everything that will happen until the end of time, both good and bad. On a personal level, He knows our deepest thoughts and intentions, even before we know those things ourselves. He knows what we will do, say, and think, every hour of every day. He already knew you would say what you said or think what you thought. None of our private thoughts are secret from Him. He knows them all.

I hate to break it to you, but not even church behavior is secret from God. We can play our friends, even church folks, but we can't play the God of Abraham, Isaac, and Jacob. No one can deceive Him. He cannot be bought, paid off, or manipulated. And no one can mislead Him—ever.

The truth is that nothing is hidden from the God we say we worship. He is aware of everything going on in your life and mine. He doesn't need to gather facts from our friends, neighbors, coworkers, or relatives to discover what's going on with us. In fact, it should comfort us to know God is already well aware of everything about us, inside and out. None of it surprises Him, because He knows us so very well. He created us. Psalm 139 says it best:

> You have searched me, LORD, and you know me. You know when I sit and when I rise; you perceive my thoughts from afar. You discern my going out and my lying down; you are familiar with all my ways. Before a word is on my tongue you, LORD, know it completely. You hem me in behind and before, and you lay your hand upon me. Such knowledge is too wonderful for me, too lofty for me to attain. Where can I go from your Spirit? Where can I flee from your presence? If I go up to the heavens, you are there; if I make my bed in the depths, you are there. If I rise on the wings of the dawn, if I settle on the far side of the sea, even there your hand

will guide me, your right hand will hold me fast. If I say, "Surely the darkness will hide me and the light become night around me," even the darkness will not be dark to you; the night will shine like the day, for darkness is as light to you. (1–12)

Interestingly enough, as great as it is that we know God, it's even more incredible to realize that He knows us intimately. And though He knows all our limits, our weaknesses, and our issues, He is still madly, passionately in love with us— enough that He sent His Son to die in our place, to restore an exquisite relationship between us and Him.

For instance, imagine a human father coming home from work, eager to get a glimpse of his adorable toddler son. He opens the door, sees his little boy, and smiles from ear to ear, with pride lighting up his eyes. Then he bends down, reaches out and says, "Come to Daddy, baby boy!" The boy's eyes light up as he runs into the arms of his father, who never fails to dote on his every move. The father believes the very best of his child and wants to bless him in everything he does, every moment of every day.

This is God. He wants the very best for you.

> Nothing in all creation is
> hidden from God's sight.

Hebrews 4:13 says, "Nothing in all creation is hidden from God's sight. Everything is uncovered, exposed and laid bare—before the eyes of him to whom we must give account." How many others do you have in your life who know all your faults and shortcomings and still love you unconditionally? They're very rare, aren't they? Even those who believe they know you—your husband, your parents, your best friend, your prayer partner—may not truly know you. But God knows you inside and out. He even knows the number of hairs on your head (Luke 12:7). Those minute details are important to Him. Clearly, no one else knows you that well.

God gets you. He knows your actions, your personal flaws, your limitations, and your motivations. He's well aware of your strengths and abilities. He knows your shortcomings, your human failures, and even your secret sins. He knows which ones you've confessed and which ones you haven't mentioned yet. He knows things about you that you yourself are not aware of. He knows what you're good at and what you can't do. He knows if you're willing to go the distance and believe Him for the impossible. He knows if you'll be a lying believer or a lazy saint. He knows it all. He is even able to turn those negatives into positives for His glory—if you let Him!

God isn't limited the way we humans are. He doesn't have attention deficit disorder, nor is He handicapped, because nothing slips His mind. Remember, His presence is everywhere at once, and He is not limited by distance or time.

It doesn't take long before we realize that we will never be able to wrap our minds around the entire truth of God and His ways. If we could predict His next moves and timing, He would be a small God indeed. That is not who He is. He operates from a divine blueprint, knowing the beginning from the end. He sees the entire story of our lives and loves to delight us by turning around for good what our enemy, the devil, means for our harm. More than that, He loves working side by side with us, using our talents to win the lost and reveal His incredible love for others.

In this drama we call life, God is the executive Director of what happens behind the scenes that no one else knows. And whether we want to believe it or not, His ways are perfect. His timing is flawless, always just in the nick of time to serve His purposes and reveal His glory.

In Genesis 22, we read the story of Abraham and Isaac. At a very old age, Abraham had no heirs to carry on his legacy, though God had long ago promised that his name would be made great. God had promised to make of Abraham's seed a great and mighty nation; through them, all the earth would be blessed.

> If He said it, it will happen. If He spoke it, He will back it up and make it a reality.

Through this scripture passage, we see promises of God's faithfulness. If God said it, we find that it did indeed come to pass, just as it will for us. If He said it, it will happen. If He spoke it, He will back it up and make it a reality. If He declared or decreed it, it will be a done deal. Over time, I've learned that if God wants something to happen in our lives, He will speak it into existence before it ever becomes a reality, and often long before we ever thought of it.

Remember that little phrase "God said it, I believe it, that settles it"? It's truly apropos for this moment in time. He always initiates what He orchestrates—in fact He has a track record unrivaled for speaking things into existence. In Genesis, we see how He spoke creation into existence with mere thoughts and words, and it happened just as He prophesied.

His Word is full of His demonstration as Promise Keeper extraordinaire. No one does it like He does. He speaks and it comes to pass. It's simple, not at all complicated. And although it may not happen on our timetable, His plans will never fail or be late.

God did indeed say it, and then He did it. He said it, and it was so. And because He spoke it, it became manifest, a reality. Those who know Him intimately and know His unfailing character can rest easy, knowing He's got their back.

At times, we know we've heard those promises in our spirit, but we can't see them yet. So know this: just because you can't see them doesn't mean they're not yours. When God speaks at any point in time, we can take those promises to the bank of heaven and declare that they belong to us, if only we choose to believe what He said.

If God spoke it to your spirit, choose to believe that it's already yours. Then speak, declare, and decree it with everything in you, refusing to doubt for a moment, because doubt is the cankerworm that steals our promises if we allow it. God is a "right now" God. Everything that was ever created was conceived in the mind of God before the foundations of the earth were formed.

The marvelous truth is that no devious demon can block it. No demonic pressure can override it. No witchcraft, fortune teller, or negative word can stop the promises of God from being fulfilled, because nothing and no one can stop the providential plan of God.

CHAPTER 12

Promise of Milk and Honey

"And the LORD said, 'I have surely seen the affliction of my people which are in Egypt and have heard their cry by reason of their taskmasters; for I know their sorrows. And I am come down to deliver them out of the hand of the Egyptians, and to bring them up out of that land unto a good land and a large, unto a land flowing with milk and honey; unto the place of the Canaanites and the Hittites, and the Amorites, and the Perizzites, and the Hivites and the Jebusites'" (Exodus 3:7–8 KJV).

In the case of Israel, I want us to focus on the big picture. God had already envisioned His nation of Israel, whose numbers eventually grew greater than all the sands of the sea. During the time Abraham lived, he had long ago heard the voice of God making this prophetic promise. Yet the promise was taking much longer than he had anticipated to become a reality. In fact, it took so long that Abraham fell for the lie that God had forgotten it entirely.

As a result, he and his wife Sarah came up with a plan to circumvent God's promise, to bring forth the longed-for heir. That in itself is a sermon we dare not miss. Even if God's promise seems lost to us, we dare not try to make it happen in the flesh, because that will never produce the incredible blessing God had in mind when He created and promised it. In fact, the outcome is often the exact opposite of that blessing when man meddles with God's plans.

Think of it this way: during Abraham's time, there was no nation of Israel, only one man, without a single heir. Israel at that time did not exist except in the mind of God. He had chosen Abraham because He trusted him and knew that by the power of God, Abraham would be equal to the task. Abraham simply believed God for the manifestation of the promise.

As an aside here, we can take a lesson, knowing that we dare not act unwisely toward anyone, because that person might be the singular path leading to the fulfillment of our promise. Scripture says that we might even be entertaining angels unaware (Hebrews 13:2).

As Abraham's story unfolds, God finally gives him a son, when Abraham and his wife are far past the normal age of childbearing. So it's clear that God's promise required a miracle of conception, strength, and energy for the birthing and raising of that child to adulthood. Over the next two generations, Isaac, the promised son, had a son of his own by the name of Jacob, who then produced twelve sons of his own. One of those sons, Joseph, became God's chosen representative to save the nation from starvation during a severe drought and famine. However, in the end, Joseph's family stayed in Egypt well past God's due date to leave. In time, they and their Jewish brethren became oppressed and enslaved by the pharaoh of Egypt.

During the time of their enslavement, the Israelites were exceedingly fruitful. Over a 430-year span, they became so numerous that the land overflowed with their numbers. Exodus 12:37 says their fruitfulness resulted in over six hundred thousand men, not including women and children. In the end, God's promise of numbers greater than the sands of the sea manifested within a mere 430-year span—an incredible result indeed, and the fulfillment of the covenant God had prophesied when He promised to multiply Abraham's seed so many years earlier.

The reigning pharaoh watched as God's chosen people multiplied, and became jealous enough to want to destroy them because of God's great favor on them. Their vast numbers threatened a possible takeover. In fact, by that time the Israelites far outnumbered the Egyptians. In the end, they had no other choice but to grow, because of the promise God had made to Abraham.

> If God has planned for you to succeed, you will advance to the top every time, right before those who tried to hinder your progress.

Trust me when I say that if God has a plan for you to succeed, you don't ever have to worry about your enemy and his evil plans. You never have to fret that anyone in your camp will try to stop your growth, progress, advancement, or success in the kingdom of God. If God has planned for you to succeed, you will advance to the top every time, right before those who tried to hinder your progress.

While they were in Egypt, the children of Israel had no idea that they were multiplying as a result of the promise being fulfilled. The truth is that they could see nothing but their own abject misery and heartache, much like we do when we're in an ongoing state of distress.

The Israelites had no idea that, while they were being afflicted and oppressed, the covenant was going forward—the promise was in the process of being fulfilled. During that time of oppression, they had no idea that they were being transformed into God's promised covenant nation. They had no idea that they were being made into a great nation, about to step into their incredible God-given identity.

At that point, they could only see themselves as slaves. However, God didn't see them as slaves. He saw the bigger picture. He saw their end, and it was a good one. He already saw their future as a great nation that would be a blessing to the whole world.

Nothing has changed for us. God always sees the bigger picture when He looks at us. Romans 4:17 says, "He calleth those things which be not as though they were." That's why we dare not limit ourselves or others by what we see with our eyes today. We need to leave the future up to God and trust Him to bring to pass those good plans He has for us, without being a hindrance to His promises.

Something to keep in mind: God doesn't always operate the way we think He should or hope He will. Sometimes He takes us around the mountain a few times to get us ready for better things—His ultimate purpose. In the case of the children of Israel, God had to take time to position them to receive what He had promised. He had to multiply their numbers so they could become that great nation. In fact, He allowed Pharaoh to set cruel taskmasters over them to afflict them. At that point, their bondage was too staggering to endure, and they felt stuck, trapped and hopeless. They simply couldn't bear it any longer.

Though they didn't know it at the time, God knew exactly what they were going through. None of those things were a surprise to Him. God knew their afflictions, their pain, and their trouble would cause them to cry out to God. He'd already predicted it. He is omniscient. He is well aware of how much you can handle. He also knows exactly how much you can take before you break.

In the end, the Israelites cried out to God. Have you ever been so broken that you curled up on the floor and wept as if there were no tomorrow, crying out to God for help because you had no answers? The Israelites were in that place where they were at their wits' end, without hope or answers. From that place, they cried out, "Lord, help us! We need your help.

We're broken and wounded, surrounded by the enemy, and going down for the third time. We're backed into a corner with no way out. Our backs are against the wall. Deliver us. Come to our rescue. We can't take it! This is too much for us!" They cried out to God, and I am glad God heard those desperate cries of the righteous! It gives us hope to know that He comes through for those who cry out for His help.

The Bible says, "Their cry came up unto Him" (Exodus 2:23). God heard their groaning. It wasn't just any cry—it was the cry of the very seed of Abraham. And God showed up and stepped right onto the scene. Psalms 34:19 says, "Many are the afflictions of the righteous, but God delivers us out of them all."

Let me remind you right now that God has heard your cry, and He is getting ready to deliver you. He's not sleeping on the job. He has seen your affliction. He knows exactly what you've been dealing with and is well aware of your story.

> This season is not a coincidence. Just wait until you see what comes next.

God says, "I've seen the hurt, the pain. I saw you when they mistreated you. I saw you when they stepped on you. I saw your tears, your desperate disappointment, and your endless, sleepless nights." He says, "I've seen your afflictions.

I saw what you went through to get here. You survived the gossip, the criticism, and the misunderstanding. But the more they endeavored to destroy you, the more you multiplied. You survived the plans of the liars, the haters, and the faultfinders. I was there, and I saw it all. I was not trying to kill you, nor was I trying to break you. I could've stepped in at any time, but it took time to make you into who I had already said you were—someone I could use for My glory. I designed and built you for this moment. You didn't get into this position by accident. You are not a leader by mere chance. You are not in the ministry by mistake. You are not the business owner by default. I ordered you here. This season is not a coincidence. Just wait until you see what comes next."

I want to emphasize this point again, because it's easy to believe we've lost our way from God's plan and that things will never get any better than they are today. Well, let me tell you—you and I can stop limiting God and simply choose to believe our end will be better than our beginning. At least that's what my Bible says! Haggai 2:9 says, "The latter glory of this house will be greater than the former, says the LORD of Hosts."

I know you've heard this before, but such challenging places are simply steppingstones to greatness if we keep on believing He is in control and knows the way.

At this point, we see a prophetic encounter forming on the behalf of the Israelites. God said, "Now that you have become what I want you to be, here is the exit plan—let's get you out of Egypt." The Bible says He remembered His covenant with Abraham, Isaac, and Jacob. He remembered how He had promised to bless them and to make them a blessing. So God spoke to their leader. He didn't go to the usher, the deacon, or the worship leader. He spoke to their leader. He said, "It is enough. I'm coming down. I have come down to deliver them out of the hands of the Egyptians."

God travels downward from heaven to where we are on earth. He comes to where we are. He came down when they cried out to Him, because it's true that when the praises go up, blessings come down.

God has a good memory. He never forgets His promises to you. He is the original Promise Keeper. He will never violate His own nature. He will do exactly what He says. The promises of God are all yea and amen. If He said it, it will come to pass. If He said it, we should expect it to happen exactly as He said. God said, "I'm coming down to deliver you. When I come down, I'm going to shift your season. I'm taking you to a good land, a large land flowing with milk and honey. And when you get there, you will taste and see that the Lord is good. So stop crying, begging, and feeling sorry for yourselves, because good things are just ahead. I'm about to make your end a good one."

I know it looks bad, but it's only temporary. So stop

grieving. Get up, wash your face, and allow great expectation to fill your heart, knowing this is only the beginning.

I know it looks like you're losing, it looks like a disaster, and it looks like you're going under, but God is going to make it good.

CHAPTER 13

Provision in the Promise

Many Christians are lacking what they need because they haven't discovered where God's provision is. It is in His promises. To receive your provision, you must know the promises of God. And you must know how to claim them—how to move in and possess them.

You and I live in a time of much uncertainty about tomorrow. We do not know what the future holds for America's economy or that of other nations. Yet thank God that we as believers in Christ have been given an incredible promise of provision—particularly in a time when provision seems so scarce. Consider the words of King David in Psalm 37: "I have been young, and now am old; yet I have not seen the righteous forsaken, nor his descendants begging bread" (Psalm 37:25 ESV). I can personally attest to the truth of this verse.

The Israelites escaped captivity in Egypt only to face the challenges of the desert. One of the biggest challenges for such a large group of nomads was finding enough food to eat. Over and over again, God provided supernaturally for His people. If God could provide for many thousands of Israelites in the middle of a desert, He can surely provide for your and your family's needs. One of the precious testimonies of Scripture is, again, David's observation: "I have been young, and now am old, yet I have not seen the righteous forsaken or his children begging for bread" (Psalm 37:25).

But even with God's supernatural provision, the Israelites still complained and grumbled in the desert. They longed for the food they had left behind in Egypt. God was literally providing bread from heaven—enough for each day—but they wanted His provision a different way. They wanted it their own way.

The actual process by which Israel moved into the land began with their first two successes, which came through miracles. A miracle opened the way for them to cross the River Jordan, and through another miracle they captured the first city, Jericho. But listen carefully—after that, they had to fight for all the rest. God said, "Every place on which the sole of your foot treads, I have given it to you" (verse 3). The only way they gained experiential possession was by actually placing their feet on the ground they were claiming. God said, "....I will bring you up out of the affliction of Egypt unto the land of the Canaanites, and the Hittites, and the Amorites, and the Perizzites, and the Hivites, and the Jebusites, unto a land flowing with milk and honey" (Exodus 3:17). God is basically said to them, "I'm coming where you are—to take you to a good land. I'm going to come and take you to myself, to make sure you don't get lost. I'm going to take you to a land flowing with milk and honey" (Deuteronomy 8:7).

My question is "Why milk? Why honey?" I have never had milk and honey together. I've had milk and doughnuts. I've had milk on my cereal. I've had honey in my tea and honey on my biscuit. But I have never had milk and honey together. Why does the Scripture mention these two food items when referring to the Promised Land?

Milk has been a staple of the human diet for thousands of years, and its significance is not lost in the pages of the Bible. Milk is mentioned in the Old and New Testaments in various contexts as a powerful symbol of abundance, spiritual nourishment, fertility, and life (Exodus 3:8).

The scriptures in the Old Testament suggest that milk was used as a staple food. According to Genesis 18:8, Abraham offered milk to the three visitors who came to him at the Oaks of Mamre and brought him news about having a son. In Song of Solomon 5:1, the man says to the woman that he entered his garden and is eating honey and drinking wine and milk. In Judges 5:25, we're told that Sisera asked for water but was offered milk by Jael. Additionally, milk was one of the foods that God promised the Israelites would find in the land of Canaan. In Exodus 3:8, God tells Moses that He has descended to free the Israelites from the Egyptians and get them to a spacious territory, a land of milk and honey, the region of the Canaanites, Hittites, Amorites, Perizzites, Hivites, and Jebusites.

In my study, I found that milk represents wealth, because only the wealthy could afford it. It represents wealth for which we didn't work. It reproduces and flows. It's a natural resource. Milk also has ties to fertility. "Fertility" refers to fruitfulness, richness, productivity, and prosperity. It also refers to abundance, which means having all we need and more than enough to share. Whatever you need, God will supply. That's why there's no need to cry over spilled milk—there's always more where that came from. Milk represents blessings. It represents the physical and spiritual sustenance that comes from God's provision and care for His people.

The land of Canaan, which God promised to the Israelites, is described as a land of milk and honey (Exodus 3:8; Deuteronomy 31:20; Jeremiah 32:22). This suggests that God's provision is abundant and overflowing. Moreover, Isaiah 55:1 urges all those who are thirsty to come to the waters, and those who have no money to come and eat—to buy wine and milk without money and without cost. This passage suggests that God's provision is abundant and freely given to those who seek it.

> In the Bible, honey is often associated
> with God's land and rescue.

The next question is "Why honey?" In the Bible, honey is often associated with God's land and rescue. The Promised Land flowed with milk and honey, and honey became a metaphor for the abundance and blessings that God bestows upon His people. Honey represents the fulfillment of His promises and His abundant provision for those who trust in Him.

Honey is also linked to the Word of God. In the book of Psalms, the psalmist declares that God's teachings are sweeter than honey. Just as honey brings joy and pleasure to our taste buds, the teachings and commandments of God bring delight and satisfaction to our souls. They are a source of wisdom, guidance, and nourishment for our spiritual lives.

One of the most significant references to honey in the Bible is its association with God's promises. The land flowing with milk and honey symbolizes the fulfillment of divine promises and the abundance of blessings that await those who remain faithful to God. It serves as a powerful reminder of God's faithfulness and His provision in every season of life. Honey in the Bible holds deep symbolic meaning, representing abundance, provision, the sweetness of God's love, and blessings.

The mention of honey in relation to the Promised Land signifies the bountiful provision and goodness that God has in store for those who trust in Him. This portrayal highlights God's intention to bless His people abundantly and fulfill His promises of prosperity and provision. The mention of honey serves as a reminder of the goodness and faithfulness of God to His children.

> Honey represents what your enemy
> is gathering for your good.

In case you didn't know it, honey also represents what your enemy is gathering for your good. Proverbs 13:22 (NKJV) says, "The wealth of the sinner is stored up for the righteous." It's talking about the honey dimension. Bees make more honey than they need. The bees know that their winter survival depends on having a source of food and they will not be particularly eager to give up the harvest! If you try to take it from them, they will sting and kill you. But they are working, putting all the ingredients together to create honey for your use. They labor, working hard, and you are the beneficiary of their hard work.

My friend. I'm writing to remind you that you're on your way to a land where you'll benefit from your enemies' actions. You will benefit from the hard labor of someone else. Your enemy is gone, after putting in the work. You will benefit. God said, "I'll prepare you a table in the presence of your enemies" (Psalm 23:5).

God said, "And I am come down to deliver them out of the hand of the Egyptians, and to bring them up out of that land unto a good land and a large, unto a land flowing with milk and honey..." Speaking to Moses from a bush burning with miraculous fire, God promises two actions in this verse. First, He has "come down" to deliver the nation of Israel from the Egyptians. The idea of "coming down" likely connects with the plagues He would later use against the Egyptians. This is a statement evoking the image of a powerful king coming off of His throne in order to wield His power. Second, God will "bring them up" from Egypt into a new land. The land God intends to bring Israel into was "up" in the sense of being at a generally higher elevation from sea level but is also a significant improvement from their state in slavery. This verse is the first to present a description repeated throughout the Torah. It is a good land, a "broad land"—meaning large—it is "flowing with milk and honey," and it was occupied by six other nations at that time. The phrase "milk and honey" refers to a land full of good things, including food for the Israelites. This was in contrast with the desert region of Egypt where milk and honey were difficult commodities to obtain.

Milk and honey symbols evoke the Promised Land, a place of richness and promise for God's chosen people.

Milk is abundant life.

Milk is another word for joy.

Milk signifies plenty.

Honey is good pleasure.

Milk is wealth.

Honey is the sweetness of life.

Milk is increase.

Honey is happiness.

Milk is massive gain.

Honey is God's good pleasure to give to us to reveal and use for God's glory.

Milk is prosperity.

Honey is delight.

Milk indicates riches.

So the God who knows all things pairs milk and honey together, because together they represent completeness and wholeness, wholeness and agreement.

Milk and honey are symbols of prosperity.

Milk and honey represent overflow.

Milk and honey include all good things.

Milk and honey symbolize God's goodness.

The word *shalom* means "peace." It also means "nothing missing or broken."

In conclusion, I prophesy over you this Word of God. God says, "When I deliver you this time, when I bring you out this time, when I heal you this time, when I make a way this time, get ready for flow. It's going to start flowing milk and honey, endlessly, with no more lack and no more shortages. I promised Abraham that I would bless his seed. And you are the seed of Abraham. All these blessings shall come upon you to do the work of the kingdom and glorify your God."

When you've got milk and honey, blessed shall you be in the city and in the country.

When you've got milk and honey, blessed are you going out and coming in.

When you've got milk and honey, the Lord will command the blessing on, over, around, and through you.

When you've got milk and honey, you are the head and not the tail.

God will bless all the work of your hands.

The land of milk and honey is a prophetic season: a season of promise, a land of goodness, a land of provision. Your next blessing will not be an accident. Your next blessing will not be a slipup.

So start decreeing these things. Say, "My season has changed. I am in a new and fresh start, a new land, for which I give thanks and praise for provision. I give You glory. May our seed be used to bring shelter to the homeless, comfort to the sick, and rest to the weary. Amen and amen."

Now stick with me while I turn the corner, because I don't want you to miss this: There's only one thing that can prevent God's plans from manifesting in reality, and it's a key we often neglect—*one that we ourselves control*. James 1:6 (ESV) says, "Ask in faith with no doubting, for the one who doubts is like wave of the sea and tossed." James 1:8 (NIV) notes that a person should not expect to receive anything from the Lord, for "such a person is doubleminded and unstable in all they do." To be double-minded is to be double-souled or double-hearted, to exist with divided loyalties and allegiances. Double-minded people are easily swayed by doubt or uncertainty, which is the opposite of a follower of God. We cannot be double-minded in our faith if we want to receive the promise of milk and honey.

God says that doubt is the opposite of faith and ties the hands of God so that He can do nothing on our behalf, even if we say we agree with Scripture. What a terrible situation for Him, who is all-powerful! Our negative words and thoughts are the only things that prevent God from accomplishing miracles, signs, and wonders in the lives of those He cherishes—you and me. Not only that, but negativity hinders us from revealing the glory of God. If we agree with doubt, thinking that what looks impossible will never happen in our lives, how can we possibly shout to the world that God is good and loves them unconditionally?

Think of it this way: the earth was created by the thoughts and words of God, which were completely in sync, without a bit of doubt. Well, it's our responsibility to examine our hearts for negative thoughts and words, and then cancel them out with our faith, saying, "I cancel unbelief, doubt, and disappointment and replace every single one of them with faith. Miracles, signs, wonders, healing, and even resurrections are my legacy. I refuse to let go of them until they manifest in my life."

In conclusion, the connection between milk and honey and the Promised Land is evident throughout the Bible. God promises to provide milk and honey to His chosen people as a sign of His provision. The promise emphasizes His desire to bless them with abundant life. Deuteronomy 26:9 (NIV) echoes this promise: "He brought us to this place and gave us this land, a land flowing with milk and honey." It reaffirms that God fulfills His promises and provides for His people's needs.

Beyond their literal meaning, milk and honey also hold spiritual significance. They represent the sweetness and nourishment of God's Word and presence. Just as milk nourishes and honey sweetens, God's provision and blessings enrich the lives of His followers.

FINAL WORD

In the story of Jacob's ladder in Genesis 28, Jacob caught the angel of the Lord going up and down the ladder. Jacob refused to let the angel go until the angel blessed him. You and I can do the same thing. In fact, we must. We must get fired up, knowing that God's promises already belong to us. They always have, since the Trinity got together and formed the plan. We can choose to speak words of hope and declare that those things God says are already ours. In fact, we should be filled with great expectations regarding God's promises. We should use those promises to bless others so that they can see the marvelous love and glory of God.

Romans 4:17 makes this profound statement: "Call those things that be not as though they were."

When we keep our eyes on His face, listen to His voice, and do what He says without doubt or wavering, He will absolutely get behind those things, because He's the source of those thoughts and plans in the first place. He cannot deny His own will and desires.

God doesn't want us to simply live in fear, doubt, dread, or disappointment—destitute like the Prodigal Son, who was in fact a rich man's entitled heir. Rather, God wants to give us the kingdom, lock, stock and barrel. In the process of changing our minds about these things, we will kick aside sadness and hope deferred, and start dancing in the streets as we get a giant, overflowing dose of joy and anticipation. He's on top of the situation and has all our bases covered, no matter how it looks to the human eye. As Scripture says, He never fails.

That means we're not just allowed but commanded to speak things into being, to make them happen—things that have yet to see the light of day—just by declaring what we hear God say.

Why don't we do these things? Because of past disappointments and belief in the devil's lies that say we don't deserve them or that God isn't as good as His Word. But that's not who we are. We are King's kids, endowed by the DNA of our wonderful Father, to be His hands extended on the earth. We're not to settle for second best, agreeing with the devil when he lies about our identity, our capabilities, or our inheritance.

In fact, I'm already seeing these things take form in the lives of those around me, as I speak these things, not only in my own life but in the lives of those I love. They report that they're seeing improvement in mobility, flexibility, strength, and endurance as I agree with them in prayer and decrees. One of my friends signed up with a wellness center to increase the blood flow to her cold feet. In the process, she's been using these spiritual tools and even visualizing better blood flow. This is increasing the circulation to her legs and feet and telling the pain to go, because it's a lie of the devil. This therapy is supposed to take a total of twelve weeks, and she's already very much improved in the fourth week. Wow.

Imagine what would happen if we all chose to shatter doubt and anxiety about promises that we have yet to see! It just requires us to let go of compromise, refuse any iota of doubt, and drag faith into every cell of our being. Then we decree what God says, believing it is absolute.

If that hasn't happened yet, we haven't completely sold out to God's good plans for us. Rather, we have left room for the enemy to sneak in and steal what is rightfully ours. It's up to us to slam the door on doubt and choose to believe every word God says is already ours.

Let's get it done!